Five Years to Liberty

The War Poems
of John Buxton

Five Years to Liberty

The War Poems of John Buxton

Introduction by
Murray Maclean

The Pentland Press
Edinburgh – Cambridge – Durham – USA

© Murray Maclean, 1994

First published in 1994
by The Pentland Press Ltd
1 Hutton Close
South Church
Bishop Auckland
Durham

All rights reserved.
Unauthorised duplication
contravenes existing laws.

British Library
Cataloguing in Publication Data
A catalogue record for this book
is available from the British Library.

ISBN 1-85821-251-0

Typeset by Carnegie Publishing Ltd., 18 Maynard St., Preston
Printed and bound by Antony Rowe Ltd., Chippenham

Acknowledgements

John and Marjorie were both attentive and generous godparents, who retained a lasting interest in all their godchildren.

During their lifetime they knew much more about their godchildren than we knew about them.

With their passing and, in 1995, the 50th anniversary of the ending of the Second World War, I wish to pay a small personal tribute to them and to the countless other families who were similarly affected by the trauma of separation and captivity during those years of war.

In presenting the poems and the accompanying introduction, I wish to express my sincere thanks to the following –

to the Executors of John Buxton's estate and Macmillan London, for their permission to republish the selected poems:

to Mike Berry and Bill King, both members of the Ridgeway Military and Aviation Research Group, for their help with historical research:

to the Imperial War Museum, Department of Documents, for permission to read and select information from the diary of Major E. Booth RE:

to the Imperial War Museum, Department of Photographs, for their permission to reproduce the cover photograph and photographs on pages 12, 14, 26, 48, 50, 82, and to Brian Prior (a member of the Ridgeway Military and Aviation Research Group) for the photograph on page 74:

to Valerie Petts, for the line drawings:

to Michele Bennett, for typing and presentation:

to Thérèse Fitzgerald, for cover artwork:

to my wife, who shares the memories of John and Marjorie, for her help and interest.

John Buxton as a young man, (circa) 1936

JOHN BUXTON'S WAR POETRY

PROLOGUE

John Buxton was born at Bramhall, Cheshire, on December 16th 1912, the youngest of three children. His father, Fred, was the owner of a Lancashire cotton mill which specialised in making calico and the canvas lining for Avon motor tyres.

The family prospered, moving later to a large Victorian house on the edge of nearby Wilmslow, complete with walled gardens, greenhouses and ample stabling.

John was sent to Malvern public school and thence went to New College, Oxford, in 1931 where he studied literature. He remained at Oxford, as a postgraduate, until 1936. He travelled in Europe with his parents as a schoolboy and later to Norway as a student.

To his father's considerable dismay he showed no inclination to return to the family business. While trying to make up his mind what to do, he revisited Norway to do more bird-watching and skiing. Whilst there he was introduced to the King of Norway and spent time coaching the King's son in English.

He returned to England undecided upon a career which could encompass his love of literature and poetry. So he took up a summer post as a part-time nature warden on the island of Skokholm (off the coast of South Wales), where he met his wife-to-be, Marjorie. She was the sister of the naturalist Ronald Lockley, then in charge of the bird sanctuary on the island. They fell deeply in love. John's ability to express himself, which was to become so well illustrated in his war poetry, is manifest in a few lines from a letter he wrote Marjorie when they were courting,

The War Poems of John Buxton

". . . I tried so hard to make a poem for you . . . but I couldn't, for my words seem only like little paper boats; they cannot bear all my love, or they must sink. They are too frail . . ."

War broke out soon after John and Marjorie were married and John volunteered for service in the Navy. While awaiting his call-up, he responded to the War Office appeal to all Colleges for men with special language qualifications. His earlier experience in the school Cadet Force ensured that he went straight to an OCTU at Aldershot ("Khaki"). He was there only two months before being posted, as an Intelligence Officer, to the 1st Independent Company (later to become the 1st Commandos). His knowledge of Norway and its language made him an ideal candidate for the Norwegian campaign in May 1940 ("M.B. to J.B.").

John Buxton's Poems 1940-45

The Norwegian Campaign

Part I

Opposing Illustration		Poem
1	(Blank page)	M.B. To J.B.
2	Photograph of John, in uniform, with Marjorie, April 1940	Khaki
3	Photograph of the naval attack on Narvik (I.W.M.)	The Invasion Of Norway
4	Photograph of troop ship approaching the shore in a Norwegian Fiord (I.W.M.)	Landfall
5	Drawing of a shallow grave in a spruce grove	Elegy
6	Drawing of a small mountain lake in the Norwegian landscape	The Tarn
7	Drawing of a skylark in free flight	The Prisoner To The Singing Bird
8	Drawing of a bunch of Marigolds in mid-air	To A Girl Who Threw Me Marigolds
9	Drawing of a whirlpool	I Sonnets
10	Photograph of burnt-out wooden houses in Narvik (I.W.M.)	Hemnes

THE NORWEGIAN CAMPAIGN: APRIL–JUNE 1940

Two thirds of Germany's iron ore requirement came from Scandinavia, being shipped out in freighters from the Swedish port of Luleä and the Norwegian fiord port of Narvik.

Both the British and French governments were aware that if they could cut the "iron route", Germany would soon be forced to capitulate. Churchill, as First Lord of the Admiralty, was enthusiastic to launch a naval expedition to sever this vital German raw material lifeline. France was also keen to participate in the campaign, offering her well-trained Alpine troops, who would prove well suited to fighting in Norway's arctic and mountainous terrain.

While the Allied expedition was delayed, the Germans took the initiative and invaded Norway, landing forces on April 9th at Narvik in the north, at Trondheim, and Oslo in the south. The Allies' response came with landings at Namsos, on April 16/17th, and Andalnes on April 18th. Both groups had to be withdrawn two weeks later in the face of superior German forces.

British naval action on April 13th isolated the northern German force at Narvik, allowing the Allies to land troops on the nearby island of Hinnoy ("Invasion of Norway").

It would not be until April 28th that joint British, French and Norwegian forces finally captured Narvik. The irony of this belated and limited success was that it would allow these same troops to be evacuated with relative safety ten days later.

John Buxton's part in the battle for Narvik began when No. 1 Independent Company, to which he was attached as a 2nd

THE WAR POEMS OF JOHN BUXTON

Lieutenant, was landed on the 4th May in the little port of Mo, at the head of Rainfiord ("Landfall").

They were part of a larger group, codenamed "Scissorsforce", detailed to harass the Germans advancing up the only road northwards, to relieve their forces at Narvik.

Each self-contained unit of some 20 officers and 270 men were to co-operate with the local population and the Norwegian Army. They proved unable to halt the German drive north from Mosjoën, being ill-equipped and inadequately trained to withstand the well-armed and determined units opposing them.

Their fate was sealed when they were outflanked by a German sea-borne force which landed at Hemnesberget. This small group was supported by two Dornier aircraft which first bombed the little town before landing to disembark a unit of men heavily armed with machine guns and mortars.

John Buxton's platoon, which had been guarding the town, was driven out. ("Elegy. For — killed at Hemnesberget May 10th 1940"). They tried to rejoin the rest of the Company at Mo ("The Tarn"). At Mo, the Company was attacked by Stuka dive-bombers on May 12th while being reinforced by a sea-borne landing of the Scots Guards' battalion.

The combined British and Norwegian Army units were forced to abandon the burning town, retreating northwards, harried and dive-bombed all the way to Rognan at the head of Saltfiord, where they were evacuated in the nick of time by a commandeered flotilla of small Norwegian "puffer" craft on May 20th.

John's poem "The Prisoner to the Singing Bird", written in Norway, is dated May 16th. If one assumes the date relates approximately to his capture, then he must have been taken prisoner during the retreat either to, or from, Mo.

In a poem written later ("Hemnes") he relates seeing men's homes burning, "listening to the whining bombs that fell" and to hearing other accounts of the intense conflict; all could relate to experiences at Mo.

The Allied forces were successfully evacuated by June 7th, leaving the Norwegians little option but to surrender, on June 10th. With the end of the Norwegian campaign, prisoners were moved southwards to Oslo ("To a Girl Who Threw Me Marigolds"), on their way to internment in Germany. Hunger and fatigue were to be the means by which the German authorities rendered prisoners as harmless as possible in their movement from the battlefronts to captivity.

M.B. to J.B.

My John, go if you must –
I'll never bid you stay,
But pray for you, and long for you
While you're away.

And I'll not keep you
If you must go to fight.
Ah! but I'll be lonely, John,
Each long, long night.

And I'll not stop you
Doing all you dare.
But I'll be sad at waking, John,
And you not there.

Marjorie Buxton

Note:
This poem affirming her love for him would have been an ever welcome solace in the years that were to follow.

THE WAR POEMS OF JOHN BUXTON

2nd Lieutenant John Buxton With His Wife Marjorie, Spring 1940

KHAKI

O my black feet upon the square,
My hands that stretch from khaki sleeves,
My eyes that straight ahead must stare
Nor watch the sparrows in the eaves,
How strange you have become to me
Who once of the earth was free!

Now in the khaki I'm confined,
Eyes, ears and spirit prisoners all.
My eyes that once saw beauty – blind.
My ears deaf to birds' song or call.
In this incurious world I'm held,
From my old life expelled.

Aldershot, March 1940

Note:
   He expresses his distaste for the consuming and mindless discipline of service life.

THE WAR POEMS OF JOHN BUXTON

Scenes from the range predictor post above the bridge of HMS Cairo of the bombardment and landing of troops in Narvik. (I.W.M. N.219)

The Invasion of Norway

Now among black, even spruces
And light-entangled birches,
And where heaving Glomma races,
The enemy marches.

Now from the quiet forest
The stillness is flushed and flown,
And of all its flowers the fairest,
Blåvaie is trampled down.

Soon among the splintered branches
The birds, returning from winter,
Will hear how a bullet wrenches
A man's cries fainter.

Aldershot, April 1940

Note:
    John, knowing that he has been selected for the expedition, is concerned that the wild and rugged beauty of Norway is about to be desecrated by the destruction of war.

THE WAR POEMS OF JOHN BUXTON

*Troops on board, approaching shore,
in a Norwegian fiord (I.W.M. N.61)*

LANDFALL

See, this long land has sails of snow,
And at her craggy stem
The silver sheeny water parts in slow
White waves, that cool and go
To blue again. We come
Not to admire, to know
The joy of her white solitude, to ride
With her adrift upon the breathing tide,
No, we are trespassers upon this world,
We, men in khaki, with our weapons held
Ready to kill. What right had any man
Ever to break this peace?
Here's no fit place
For our fierce rowdy farce to be performed.
Could men not leave this land unharmed?
O you indifferent mountains, ice, and snow
Forgive us where we go,
Pardon our sinfulness in bearing arms
Across this land. Then let us come again
When peace shall end this pain
Here to atone for all our sacrilege.

Norway, May 8th 1940

Note:
　His return to Norway, in uniform as part of an invasion force, is a far cry from his earlier happy visits.
　He dislikes the "rowdy farce" of invading such a beautiful and peaceful landscape; feeling that he now comes as a "trespasser", and like a Judas, has betrayed this land to those that will tarnish it with blood.

The War Poems of John Buxton

"Here in this spruce's shade . . . rest, and forget . . ."

Elegy

Rest now, rest: here's an end
    To all your pain.
Rest, while we others spend
    Our lives in vain.

Here in this spruce's shade
    Where snow lies yet,
Alone now but unafraid
    Rest, and forget.

About you the forest grows
    Careless of you.
There's nothing here that knows
    The ill men do.

Above, the white mountains rise
    Past the dark hills:
There no man lives nor dies,
    There no man kills.

Rest in this solitude,
    Rest, you who can.
No more do you intrude
    As that fool, man.

    (For —-, killed at Hemnesberget, May 10th 1940)

Note:
    He shows his anger at the futile waste of a life, and that such beauty is sullied by man's foul deeds to man.

"Keep behind the trees, down to the tarn's edge . . ."

The Tarn

"We'd better split now. Keep behind the trees
Down to the tarn's edge. If there's a plane, come back
And meet me here: don't fire, they'll have MGs.
– We'll need to get as close as we can get."
I heard the silky rustle of the skis
And stood stock-still, listening till it had gone.
I threaded one stick through the ring and strap
Of the other, and held them so in my left hand.
I cocked my tommy-gun – so loud, so loud
That little click! Zigzag from tree to tree,
Straining for any other sound beyond
The swishing of my skis, I ran to the tarn.
Between the black, still branches of a spruce
I looked across the ice: only the wind
Had made black random furrows in the snow.

Note:
   He describes vividly the reality of being in combat; decisions, fears and the tensions of action.
   The pulse races as the poem matches the pace of his adrenalin.

THE WAR POEMS OF JOHN BUXTON

"The singing bird"

The Prisoner to the Singing Bird

Sing on, sing on beyond the walls
That I within may know
Spring is in the woods again
Where you may go.

Sing on, sing on; then in my cage
I shall delight to hear
That you are glad and free out there –
So near, so near!

Norway, 16th May 1940

Note:
   Just over a week after landing he was a prisoner, and had thus become one of the first English POWs. Little did he know that he would have to wait for five long and hungry years before he too would be "free out there".

"Marigolds"

TO A GIRL WHO THREW ME MARIGOLDS

"Throw your yellow marigolds
Nor ask yourself why –
There's no one here about you
Half so proud as I.

Throw your yellow marigolds
To this prisoner me –
These Germans with their rifles
Are not half so free.

Throw your yellow marigolds
For I am young and tall,
And I am an Englishman.
– Look! I hold them all!"

(Oslo station, June 1940)

Note:
  He is proud to be English, even though now a prisoner. He goes into captivity with head held high.

The War Poems of John Buxton

"Amid the whirl of anger, fear and shame . . ."

SONNETS

I

I was a captive too while yet uncaught:
  I held that men but by mistake did ill –
  And helped to punish them, thought guiltless still.
I had no freedom, yet for freedom fought.
I left my joyful love, and hatred sought,
  And wishing men to live, I tried to kill;
  And so, unwilling to obey my will,
Forsook my duty to do what I ought.
No, there's no answer, though I think and think.
  War's Chaos; and no man can Cosmos frame
    Unless he flings his soul in the ruin there.
Then must he stand and watch, and watch it sink
  Amid the whirl of anger, fear, and shame;
    And like a patient madman he must stare.

Summer 1940, Oflag VII C, Germany

Note:
He begins the painful process of self-analysis – he realises that he was already "imprisoned" by his necessary involvement in duty and service to his King and Country – carrying out orders which were alien to his own sense of right and wrong.

*All that remained of one of Narvik's houses occupied by the Nazis
(I.W.M. N.269)*

2

HEMNES

I saw men's homes burst into sudden flower
   Of crimson petals round each golden shell.
   I listened to the whining bombs that fell
And felt the hard earth shudder at their power.
I saw bewildered eyes that hour by hour
   Had peered through rifle sights. I heard men tell
   How many rounds they fired. I learned, the smell
Of cattle burning in the byres is sour.
So much war taught me. And, when I return,
   Because I did not cower nor shirk the fight,
   But took a little part in this mad play,
Because I too have helped to kill, wreak, burn –
   "You did your duty, helped defend the right,
   You too were brave," some poor, blind fool
     will say.

Oflag VII C, Germany

Note:
   Painful memories continue to haunt him.
   He is increasingly conscious that he has been a party to deeds which are completely alien to his peace-loving nature. He detests the 'cheap' excuse of absolving his guilt by saying that it was all done in the name of "duty".

CAPTIVITY IN GERMANY
PART II

Opposing Illustration	Poem
11 A map of POW camps in Europe	*Close Up the Map*
12 Photograph of Laufen Castle taken from the river (I.W.M.)	*The River Runs Fast*
13 Laufen 'Camp' parade ground with trees (I.W.M.)	*Lime Tree*
14 Picture of a harebell	*Harebell*
15 Photo of John (centre) and Marjorie on Skokholm island	*Dedication to 'Westward'*
16 Photo of the watercolour	*Berries*
17 (Poem covers both pages)	*Lines on re-Reading Robert Bridges' The College Garden in 1917*
18 A wartime drawing of the camp showing the trees and bird nest boxes	*The Apple Trees*
19 Silhouette of a soldier	*Sonnets 5*
20 (Blank Page)	*Sonnet*
21 Drawing of bombers in the night sky	*Night Raid*
22 (Blank page)	*Sonnets 8 (If for a Single Hour . . .)*

23	Photograph of US bombers leaving white daylight vapour trails	*Daylight Raid*
24	Line drawing of John by R. Bagot, 1943	*Sonnets 2*
25	Photograph of Harold Speed's drawing of Marjorie	*On Receiving Harold Speed's Portrait of M.B.*
26	POW photo of prisoners skating at Eichstaëtt (I.W.M.)	*Walking in the Snow*
27	A picture of a willow warbler	*Willow Warbler*
28	A drawing of a seashore	*On Seeing the Sea for the First Time for Five Years*
29	(Blank page)	*II – Sonnets 8*

CAPTIVITY IN GERMANY
JUNE 1940-MAY 1945

John Buxton was to spend the rest of the war in a series of POW camps deep in Germany. In captivity his poetry took on real purpose as he began to express his feelings about the events which had befallen him.

He arrived at Laufen camp in late June 1940 where he joined other British officers captured at Dunkirk. In the absence of any written or verbal information from John about his time in captivity, the following account has been drawn from the diary of Major E. Booth RE who arrived at Laufen at the same time as John. The two men were to spend the rest of the war in the same camps. They were moved from camp to camp at the same time, because both had surnames beginning with 'B', which placed them in the same batch in their moves from Laufen to Warburg in October 1941, and a final move to Eichstaëtt in September 1942.

Throughout John's captivity Marjorie continued to live in their cottage at Long Crendon in Buckinghamshire. She joined the Women's Land Army, working on the farm at the end of her street. Her employer let her off work as much as he could, so that she could go to Red Cross meetings. She became involved at a high level in the organisation of the parcels sent out to prisoners in Germany.

LAUFEN – OFLAG VII C/H

It had originally been the country palace of the Archbishop of Salzburg, the largest building dating back to the eighteenth century.

The palace was modernised before the war for use as a youth hostel and then converted into barracks. The main buildings ranged around two courtyards, a large pebble-paved one and another smaller one.

The main building block was on the river front, along the inner side of which was a range of stable buildings used to house the other ranks, who were employed to clean up in the camp or to go out into the fields to dig for their staple diet of potatoes.

Within the buildings there were stone-flagged corridors, overlooking the courtyards. The rooms contained up to fifty-one beds in tiers of three, all of which were occupied. Tables with benches and stools were placed down the middle of the room. There were cupboards or wardrobes, each of which was shared by three to four men. An average of 15 sq. ft. of room space per man was much lower than the British Army's minimum requirement of 35 sq. ft. By mid-July 1940 there were 1200 officers and 150 other ranks in the overcrowded camp. The overcrowding resulted in having to queue for everything, including going to the lavatory.

Their bedding consisted of a mattress filled with straw or wood-shavings, one thin blanket, one white sheet, a pillow and a blue check bag-cover for the blanket. The sheet and pillow case were changed once a month. This was inadequate bedding for hungry men in the cold winter months to follow.

Beyond these buildings lay the parade ground called 'The Great Field', surrounded by a high, double-banked wire fence overlooked by a sentry tower. The field was about 1½ acres in size. In the centre stood a large lime tree ("Lime Tree"). On one side a row of chestnut trees bounded the village street beyond the wire. On the other side the ground sloped steeply down to the river beyond a parapet wall. Austria lay beyond the river, which was crossed by a suspension bridge to the village and the Austrian Alps beyond.

A steep path led down to the river bank from the parade ground to a smaller recreation enclosure alongside the river. Barbed wire fences and a look-out tower were again present to prevent escapes.

In the early months of captivity the lack of food became an obsession with the men as their bodies slowly adjusted to the meagre diet.

The daily menu consisted of a mug of Ersatz coffee (a substitute made from oak acorns) for breakfast. Lunch was a bowl of barley soup and three potatoes followed by an early supper of flaked corn soup, again with three potatoes. This meagre, near liquid, diet was supplemented by a bread ration of one loaf per man every four to five days. The hard, brown, sour-tasting loaf was date stamped on the top; some loaves being over a month old and very mouldy upon distribution. As the months passed this old stock was replaced with fresher bread.

These early months in captivity with a very poor diet would result in lasting damage to the health of many men, including John Buxton. There were virtually no Red Cross food parcels to augment or improve the quality of their diet and when the parcel did arrive, the Germans reduced their food supply in relation to the flow of parcels, so the men continued to remain hungry, even though the content of the Red Cross parcels did improve the quality and variety of their daily food intake. The most popular item in the parcels were condensed milk and chocolate powder, which were often mixed together to make a kind of chocolate fudge.

Each POW received a little camp pay according to his rank. John, as a second Lieutenant, was given twelve marks every ten days. With this money they could buy a few extras including their allocated cigarette ration of two per day. Some inmates tried to supplement this by making their own cigarettes from a variety of leaves found in the camp grounds. Dried cherry leaves proved to be the most acceptable. Other sources such as dried potato peel, tea leaves or clover flowers were not successful.

In November 1940 the supply of Red Cross parcels dried up for a while, only to be replaced by private purchase parcels ordered from home. The contents could not be eked out over several weeks because of a German paranoia with security. They believed the food parcels were being used to smuggle in escape gear. So they ordered that the contents of all tinned or packaged foods must be opened in the presence of the guards. The contents could then be removed in any containers that the prisoner could muster. It meant that the parcel's recipient and his friends had to eat the whole lot within a few days before the food went off; so they lurched from feast and back to famine again. This diet sapped their energy, leaving them tired, listless and unenthusiastic for anything. The onset of cold winter weather was greeted with the distribution of captured, blue, Dutch army greatcoats in December, the spoils of war, yet a great help in 18° of frost.

December was also marked by the first payment of money which could be sent by relatives. Each man was allowed to receive 19 marks and 99 pfennigs, the equivalent of £2.00. This was a welcome addition to their camp pay, now increased to 24 marks, allowing them to purchase more necessities such as extra blankets. These were often converted into sleeping bags, dressing gowns or simply worn as a cape to keep out the winter's cold – on December 18th 1940 the night temperature fell to 0°F (–18°C).

Inadequate food and poor, cramped conditions led to regular bouts of gastro-enteritis sweeping the camp. At any one time 10% of the camp would be badly affected; most men suffering from the illness, on and off, on a regular basis. In January 1941 the Germans relaxed their practice of opening all the contents of food parcels, so allowing the men to consume this vital extra food steadily over a longer period.

Red Cross and YMCA representatives visited the camp to check on conditons. This resulted in Red Cross parcels arriving every week, so relieving their hunger and improving the men's physical condition at a critical time, in the midst of the winter's coldest weather. Hunger and lack of motivation had led many men to become casual and scruffy, both in their dress and personal hygiene.

Morale was further eroded by rumour, wild tales of a possible German invasion of England being the most common. These "Latrinograms", as they became called, were mostly initiated by the guards, and led to bouts of depression, or elation, amongst the inmates according to the current gossip. The Latrinograms were given added momentum by the delay in mail from England. Initially letters came very spasmodically, improving to a delay of about seven weeks and then settling down to an average three to four week delay. The reduced delay in the mail also reduced the level of camp rumour as the prisoners were reassured that all remained well with their loved ones at home.

To stimulate the men's morale and their will to win through, the Laufen "university" was created to occupy the men. Faculties were set up for languages, art, agriculture and the sciences; John Buxton helped enthusiastically to create a library which eventually reached a total of 2,000 books. Saved money was used to purchase books. Major Booth also records his pleasure at being able to work in the library, cataloguing the books. This work freed them from their crowded quarters and the endless "hubbub" of noisy voices all day long. The cramped rooms and lack of privacy affected most men, but particularly the older officers, who found it hard to adjust.

In addition to his work as a camp librarian, John Buxton encouraged other prisoners to help him with a study of the Redstart bird. He chose to study the Redstart because it bred about the camp, at Laufen and later at Eichstaëtt, and was easily recognised by sight and sound; a valuable asset when being helped by inexperienced prisoners. They put up nest boxes in areas where they were allowed to go, to encourage the birds and the study of their habits. The Redstart is a confiding bird and easy to approach. His copious notes, which now reside in the Oxford Museum of Natural History, show that this work fully absorbed him and his fellow prisoners; helping to relieve the tedium of captivity and giving them a sense of purpose in an otherwise bleak environment. This research led to the publication by Collins of "The Redstart" in 1946, one of the first of their nature monograph series.

During their fifteen months' stay at Laufen the camp saw three changes of commandant. Fortunately all three were enlightened men, who did their best to give the prisoners as much freedom as the system would allow. Beyond the problem of opening food parcels, there were other petty rules, one of which forbade prisoners from leaning out of the window; presumably in case it might be a prelude to an escape attempt. In late January 1941, a prisoner was shot dead for not responding quickly enough to a command not to lean out of a window. Such incidents affected overall morale in the camp. There were numerous and continued attempts to escape, all of which ended with the escapees being returned to the camp and 28 days' solitary confinement, within a few days. Each escape attempt was followed by a temporary loss of some privileges and extra roll-call parades, which could go on for hours.

The first major escape attempt was organised by a half a dozen "hardy lads", who dug a tunnel under the concrete floor of a basement room into the lane outside using only a screwdriver and small hammer. The soil had to be carried out at night-time in handkerchiefs!

In March 1941, most inmates received welcome clothing parcels of new uniforms and greatcoats; which allowed them to exchange their tatty battle-dress, that they had been wearing continuously for over nine months since their capture. John was not so lucky. He was still wearing the same battledress over a year after his capture. Fresh clothing sent from home did not reach him till later in the summer.

April heralded the arrival of spring, and the opening of an extension to the recreation ground, situated on a little peninsula between the main Salzach river and a small tributary. It was christened "the island"; part-covered with young birch trees, which provided a shady grove to lie under on hot sunny days ("Harebell"). These were better times after the long, cold, hungry days of the past winter. In every way conditions had improved over their first months in captivity.

The line of chestnut trees beside the parade ground came into bloom with a spectacular display of their candle-like flowers. Morale and physical condition had so improved that the men began to organise team games of hockey, football and cricket to help pass the time, and make the most of their allocated outdoor recreation. John continued to write regularly to Marjorie sending her love poems ("Dedication from 'Westward'").

Some men began to notice that they had developed a phobia about change. They felt secure and relaxed with the daily routine, but became nervous and irritable when drafts of new prisoners came or went, or when there was any change in the daily pattern of their existence – such as TB inoculation of the whole camp in mid-May.

Escape attempts continued, and continued to fail. As officers, they knew it was their duty, even in such secure captivity, to annoy and harass the camp authorities in a way that would ensure the presence of more guard troops than otherwise would be necessary. It helped to keep a few more men deployed away from the various fighting fronts.

The daily routines continued throughout the summer until one day in early October when it was announced that they would be moving to another camp.

WARBURG – OFLAG VIB

Their two days' move from Laufen started at 8.00 a.m. on Saturday 11th October 1941 when they were assembled at the station. Half the men were fortunate to be packed into third-class carriages, the rest being crammed into cattle trucks. They all had to remain in their respective wagons overnight for 2 nights. They were allowed off the train for a wash in a fountain on the Sunday morning. The train arrived at Warburg on Monday morning. Once disembarked, they were marched the four kilometres out into the flat and dreary countryside to the camp at the little village of Dussel. They came first to a small barbed-wire enclosure which contained a few dilapidated huts. This was the recreation area. The main camp beyond was a jumble of badly-built wooden huts set in a sea of mud, and contained nearly 3,000 mixed Army and RAF personnel.

Each hut contained eighteen beds in two tiers, with very little space between in the centre. The roughly built wash-house and latrines were appalling. There were two dining halls each to seat 3–400 men. At the start this was all there was on the site. The outlook was a flat, bleak landscape cut across by the barbed wire fences and mud inside. The grey dilapidated huts and dreary figures walking round and round was a very depressing situation. John kept up his morale by continuing to write poems to Marjorie ("Sonnet") who in turn wrote to him every other day even though some of her letters never reached him.

The huts, initially, were incredibly dirty and verminous with only one dim carbide lamp for lighting, to be put out at 10.00 p.m. Electric lighting came in due course. With only one small table in each hut, meals had to be eaten in rotation.

The camp lights were often extinguished at night due to local air raids, accompanied by the sound of defensive anti-aircraft fire. It was some comfort to John and the others to know that the Allies were hitting back deep into Germany ("Night Raid").

At the end of November, American inspectors from the US Embassy visited the camp and expressed in direct language their dissatisfaction with the conditions they had witnessed – overcrowded, primitive and dirty accommodation and verminous huts. The men spent much time cleaning up the whole camp. Eventually they were able to make a rugger pitch, a hockey pitch, two ice-rinks and a deck tennis area to greatly improve the miserable place.

During the depth of winter, the night temperature fell as low as -25°C, extremely cold for undernourished men living in unheated huts with limited bedclothes; the only advantages of the cold weather being excellent skating on the camp ice-rink and the absence of mud.

Their daily routine followed the same pattern day after day -

up at 8.00 a.m.	- breakfast of tea, toast and marmalade
9.15	- roll-call parade
9.45	- physical training – "PT"
10.30–11.30	- occupational therapy – lectures, etc.
12.30	- lunch – a bowl of soup and potatoes
1.30–2.30	- silent hour – rest
4.00	- tea
4.30	- roll-call parade
7.30	- evening meal – probably similar to lunch.

On March 6th (1942) the routine was upset by a major hut search

– every stick of furniture, clothing, bedding etc. was passed out through doors and windows to empty the huts – it proved an excellent opportunity to spring-clean the interiors once more!

With the arrival of spring, escape activity resumed in earnest, resulting in the usual retribution from the Germans; and the sea of mud returned with a vengeance!

Roll-calls lasted three to four hours and both the theatre and dining rooms were closed. The "Goons" (German guards) developed an unpleasant search habit. Thirty and more of them would descend upon one hut, throw out the occupants and all their belongings at any time. It might be 8.30 p.m. at night or 5.30 in the early morning and then again at 4.00 a.m the next morning – always searching for missing items, such as shovels, which could be used for escape attempts. By late July 46 escape tunnels had been dug, but only six of them had reached the outer perimeter fence. No escapees from these tunnels remained free for more than a few days.

This fever of escape activity resulted in many more early morning searches – inmates being awakened to find a German bayonet pointing at them. Mail was restricted as a further reprisal. This latter restriction was more keenly felt by men like John who found much succour in their letters from home.

In August rumours of another move to a further camp were verified. All hoped for something better.

EICHSTAËTT – OFLAG VII/B

All the men moved from Warburg went in alphabetical order, 'B's among those on September 1st 1942; a one-day move south by train. The camp site was elongated, on one side of a narrow valley. Along the upper edge, terraced out of the hillside, ran the main camp, comprising two storied buildings, each with good washrooms and latrines. Below the road extended a flat terrace playing field bounded by a lime tree avenue on the river side.

At the further end were six newly built, clean brick huts.

From the avenue 'promenade' one looked out over the barbed wire to the little river a hundred yards away. Beyond lay wooded slopes on the other side of the valley. To the right could be seen the spires and towers of Eichstaëtt town.

Across the river a little 'toy' train pulled three antiquated coaches, running through 'smiling' fields; altogether a much better existence.

Games of football, hockey, basketball, and restricted golf could be played. Men dug vegetable gardens to augment a diet which had improved since the early days of Laufen, and which was further augmented by the regular distribution of Red Cross Parcels.

Amongst those in the camp were 100 officers captured on the Dieppe raid. These men were the first to be singled out for reprisals resulting from reports of maltreatment of German POWs in North Africa. Their hands were tied together each day for the whole day. So began the "chain gang" incident. A few days later a further 250 officers, including John Buxton, were segregated and manacled in Block I from 8.00 a.m. to 9.00 p.m. each day for a year until the 23rd November 1943. Fortunately their chains were not a very tight fit. Mail was again restricted as an added reprisal.

Regardless of the improved conditions and the daily routine of handcuffing of up to 300 officers, escape attempts continued unabated right up till Christmas. The following summer witnessed the escape of 67 officers in one night from one tunnel; the best effort yet. However all were recaptured within two weeks and returned to spend time in solitary confinement.

At Eichstaëtt John and his small band of fellow ornithologists continued their detailed study of the Redstart. In the period April–May 1943 the group spent 850 hours recording the movements of one nesting pair alone. Such intense interest helped greatly to pass the time and gave a sense of purpose to their lives in captivity. The mass of detailed notes survived his time in Germany and enabled him to write up an exhaustive survey which Collins published in 1950.

In August one prisoner climbed up the perimeter wire in broad daylight and waved at the guards – at Laufen he would have been shot without hesitation, but under the changing conditions he was quietly removed to a mental hospital.

In the autumn the first batch of "Grande Blessée" – seriously ill or wounded men, were repatriated to England. The number included one of John's long-standing friends, who was later able to pass on first hand news of his condition to Marjorie.

With the approach of winter food again became short due to only half the normal Red Cross ration parcels being available, and no private food parcels were allowed. The flow of parcels improved again in the following February.

As the war began to turn in favour of the allies the German authorities began to show more respect and concern for the condition of their 'hostages', particularly those POWs of officer rank. The announcement of the first 'excursions' outside the camp confines – the first 'time out' for men who had been behind wire for $3\frac{1}{2}$ years was greeted with pleasure and relief. This act coincided with the ending of the daily shackling and confinement of officers.

By the spring of 1944 parade walks had been extended to the countryside around the camp, where John took pleasure in walking in the woods ("Walking in the Snow").

To be able to walk out freely into the countryside was a great morale boost for the average "Kriegie" (the English corruption of *Kriegsgefangener*, German for POW). They would lie out in the long grass, during late summer, watching US bombers pass overhead on their daylight raids, now with little noticeable opposition ("Daylight Raid").

No sooner had the parole walks started than they were stopped again as a reprisal against further escape attempts. The Germans became increasingly nervous following the Normandy landings.

John and many others had become very weary after 4 years in captivity; the lack of privacy and overcrowding added to their frustration. Most men had some habit, however petty, which was distasteful to his fellow inmates.

Here were intelligent men locked away with no responsibilities, no duties and no work to do. Many became obsessive about missing out on what was going on; they would join a queue without knowing what it was for!

Yet another winter arrived. Their food was reduced and reduced yet again. The flow of Red Cross and other food parcels was halved. Conditions for all Germans had become increasingly precarious as the Allies steadily pushed their troops back across Europe.

Further reprisals followed reports of alleged maltreatment of Germans in Egyptian POW camps. All mattresses and ninety per cent of all chairs and stools were confiscated.

April Fools' Day 1945 had a bitter sting in its tail for the inmates of Eichstaëtt camp. They were all lined up on the parade ground ready to be marched off to another camp further away from the approaching war zone, when a US jet flew over the camp, disappeared, and soon returned with six others. They proceeded to attack the camp with machine-gun fire. The attacks lasted over an hour, but seemed like a lifetime to the inmates as they tried to find shelter. Twelve men were killed and some others were wounded in this most unfortunate mishap. It would result in the prisoners being moved by night marches to another camp at Moosberg in Bavaria. John and his fellow prisoners were marched between 6.00 in the evening and 6.00 in the morning. During the daylight hours they lay up in barns and farm buildings. It was a strict regulation that everyone must stay inside. They were very aware, and afraid, of the overhead presence of US jets all day long.

As many as 25,000 POWs of all nationalities were gathered together at Moosberg, but plenty of Red Cross and German rations were available. They were also free to wander beyond the wire, John again walking in the woods nearby ("Willow Warbler").

The Moosberg camp was relieved by American troops of the 3rd US Army, after a short fight with local SS troops, on April 29th.

It would be nearly two more weeks of delay and frustration before John arrived home. They were evacuated on the eve of VE day in droves of Halifax aircraft, which ferried them home to an airfield north of London, where they met a hospitable reception in a flag-decorated hanger, on May 10th – five years to the day since he wrote his 'Elegy' to a friend killed at Hemnesberget in Norway:

"Rest now, rest: here's an end
To all your pain."

As John composed his poems in captivity, he had sent them home to Marjorie with his letters. She would type them out, sending a copy on to his mother together with his latest news.

Marjorie sent many of the poems to the national press; most were published by the *Sunday Times*, *Observer* and other leading magazines both in the UK and the USA. The collected poems were published by Macmillan in two booklets, *Such Liberty* 1944, and *Atropos* 1946. Marjorie was the guiding light, cajoling and encouraging to ensure that John's works reached the wider audience they deserved.

The early poems record the action and events of which he was a part. Some of the later ones are the more poignant as they trace the painful process of coming to terms with what he had done in the name of duty, yet against his inner convictions. This was a conflict fought in the minds of many men who went to war for "King and Country", unaware of the reality of what they would be required to do, and of the long-term consequences to their peace of mind – a peace which many never found.

The better war poets have long been held in high esteem. The meter of poetic verse allows the writer a greater freedom, and a degree of camouflage to express emotions without resorting to the familiar and worn superlatives of everyday speech. Thus they retain the freshness and purpose of their impact upon our conscience.

Many of the poems are straightforward love poems from a young man separated from his new bride whom he continued to love very deeply.

The War Poems of John Buxton

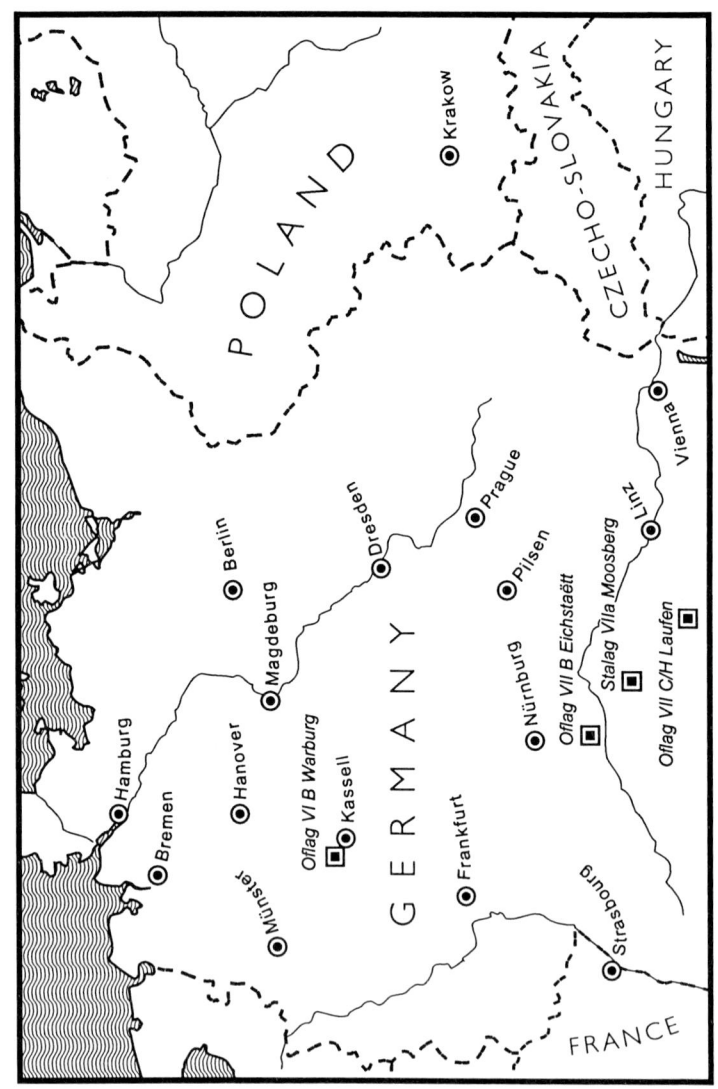

Map showing locations of the camps where John Buxton was held

Close Up the Map

Now if I lay a match along the scale
    And measure miles out on the map, how far
    These six or seven inches say you are,
How many days by water, road, and rail!
The shaded hills are dark, the valleys pale –
    A green land that black spots of cities mar,
    That criss-cross railways, roads, and rivers bar –
The lattice in the windows of a gaol!
Close up the map, for not by miles, nor days,
    Nor anything that maps or clocks can tell,
        Can love be measured, or set far, or near.
Close up the map: I see your brown eyes gaze
    Deep into mine, your tousled hair I smell,
        And all my spirit knows of you is here.

July 1940, Oflag VII C, Germany

Note:
    He muses on the distance which separates him from Marjorie – only seven inches on the map – yet seven hundred miles of land in reality.
    "Close up the map" – there is nothing to be gained by such thoughts.
    His spirit and love are strong, and yet it is early days in what were to be long years of waiting.
    The poem was published in the *Sunday Times* 7.6.42.

The War Poems of John Buxton

View of Laufen Castle from the River Salzach

THE RIVER RUNS FAST

The river runs fast
With the melted snow,
And the green leaves come,
And the dead leaves go
Hidden in the green grass
Springing up below.

The white spires of blossom
On the chestnut-trees
Are a-rumble with the wings
Of the numberless bees,
And the loud birds are back again
From Southern lands and seas.

The glad days are here now,
The bright days of sun,
And fast as the river
The spring days run –
Oh! may I be with you, my love,
Before the summer's done!

Note:
   Laufen, in the spring of 1941.
   Melting snows from the Austrian Alps, in the distance, swell the river outside the camp wire. Within, the chestnut trees reveal their dramatic "candle" blooms and his hope springs to life as well – dreaming of being home before the autumn!
   (Sent to Marjorie in May 1941.)

Laufen 1941. The prisoners on parade. (The lime tree stood, left foreground, out of the picture) I.W.M. 34252

LIME-TREE

οιη περ φυλλων γενεη, τοιη δε και ανδρων *

You are too proud, my lime-tree,
Standing in silence there,
A pillar of green, curling smoke
In motionless air.

We who walk round and round you
Like brown leaves blowing by
Remind you that in windy autumn
Your leaves will fly.

Yet why should you care, my lime-tree,
Though all your twigs are bare,
And rustling leaves blow by your feet –
Why should you care?

Note:
The lime tree stood in the centre of the main exercise area, and provided a shady focal point for the men to gather and walk around.

* Translation: "As are the leaves on the trees, so are the races of men." (Homer's *Iliad*)

"Will You Ring"

HAREBELL

Harebell! Harebell!
If I shall send
The wind to swing
Your delicate stem
When the war end
Will you ring? Will you ring?

Listen! Listen!
My bells all peal
Even now. I know
No job but the sun
And the wind that I feel
As it blows to and fro.

July 26th 1940

Note:
The analogy of the Harebell and the church bell provides a simple message; he wishes both would ring out to proclaim peace.

John (centre) and Marjorie birdwatching on Skokholm Island

Dedication from "Westward"

I see before me England, whose am I
Living, and when I die.
My names are names she gave me at the font;
I speak the speech she taught me; and, by and by,
When I was far, England was all my want.

'When I was far'! who am a prisoner now
Save as my thoughts allow
Some liberty to dream of being free,
To dream I stand on England's rocky prow
Where it thrusts Westward through the cloven sea.

Oh! I can see you standing at my side
Watching the Wild Goose tide
As you so often stood a year ago,
My dear companion, my delightful bride,
To whom all joy and all my faith I owe.

We met upon the island, you, who brought
Speech that the New World taught,
Who turned my eyes then first toward the West,
And I, who came from Norway, where I sought
Among her fells and forest strength and rest.

Later I left you for the North to fight
For things we claimed as right –
For Peace and Liberty, high-sounding names
That flaunted on our banners in men's sight.
And there we failed of all our boasting claims.

And now I cannot know where you may be
For my captivity.
But, for our love, the one thing still known true,
This poem shall be yours, who taught it me,
Turning me from the Old World to the New.

Oflag VII C/H Germany, 16th August 1940

Note:
The poem is the dedication from his long, four-part poem which was published in 1942. It is to his memories of Marjorie, during that brief period between their marriage and his departure for Norway.

'Berries' by E.M. Baumer. 1941

BERRIES

I will bring you berries
From the spinneys and the hedges,
From deep in the dark woods,
From the slow streams' edges.

I will bring you berries
From the Chiltern hills,
And from Notley mill-race
Where dark water spills.

I will bring you berries
Dusty with bloom,
And berries like lanterns
To glisten in your room.

I will bring you berries
Of juniper and yew,
Sloes from the blackthorn,
Hips whence roses grew,

And four-cleft spindle
With the orange-red pips
Shown by its cleaving
Into coral lips,

And juicy blackberries
To give a summer taste
When all the autumn
Has run to winter waste.

Oflag VII B, December 1940, Germany

Note:
Sent to Marjorie on 10.12.40 and received by her on 15.2.41. It was published in the *Observer* on 19.10.41, which resulted in a reader sending to Marjorie a beautiful water-colour which depicted a vase full of all the hedgerow flowers and fruits mentioned in the poem. Marjorie sent the picture out to John, who treasured it enough to bring it home again. It bears the camp stamp on the rear.

A LINE ON RE-READING ROBERT BRIDGES' "THE COLLEGE GARDEN IN 1917"

Far away now beyond the whining of the bombs,
Near other snows than the snows I saw about me
When the bullets trickled over the wall or flicked
The grey dust at my feet, I remember today
My loved old poet sitting "on the grassy slope
Of the old city-rampart", where I so often sat
Writing my youthful verses. He found peace that day
Basking under the limes, that some who went to war
Should yet return, and others (of whom I was one)
Should come in their turn to love the place.
    Did he fear
That we might go again to a war, who had seen the plaques
In chapel below Thomas of Deddington's glass?
One was engraved with English names, but the other one
Bore proudly there three German names. They too had
    known
The tulips flaunting by the wall, the tall tower,
And all the murky portraits hung in hall. They knew,
Perhaps remembered while they fought, the talk at nights
Of how to set the world to rights, who all were young
In peace in England.
    Ah! but war came once again
Whether he feared it or not; and again I'll see
Those plaques, old then, and others next to them, unless
The blind bombs thrust their fists in pinnacled roofs, burst

Moon-silver chambers with their gold flung a-scatter.
When last I went to chapel the windows were gone,
Buried somewhere, and in their place were boards in case
The soil should shake enough to break glass, and no more.
And after I couldn't talk for my bitten lips;
But I walked round the cloisters and saw the ilex-tree
And that old fire-engine tucked in a corner still.
    You were there, Marjorie, for whom I wrote
"Westward",
And many poems, Christopher longing to speak
Yet not knowing how, and Alan trying to smile,
And Kathleen, and the Warden's widow of three days
At whom I dared not look for my tears, though I wore
No gown but a Sam Browne then.
    I forget what more;
But now I am far from the bombs's whine, sirens' shriek,
Far from these English hours of pride, not fighting still,
Nor at peace, but useless, inert, for this time dead.
"Oh! but you fight – fool" fool! how I hate that past
    tense, fraught
With all the poor lies of those past years while we cringed.
England had known no danger when I was fighting
But slept, and awoke not by Arctic snow or fiord
But at Dunkirk. And since, who of us has fought, and died?
Ralph, he left the river for the clouds, and died there;
Oliver, with whom I walked through lost towns of Greece,
Is fighting near the bones of the men who incised
His tablets of clay and cylinders. Richard Wood
I met here: we eat soup at the same table now.
Where are the rest?
    But I'll not be always dead, like this;
I shall go back, as some will not whose names I'll learn

Carven beneath the windows (put back bit by bit).
And there may be more on the other wall, German names.
The bells that they heard, and the last war's names they read,
The grey wall, the peonies in the beds below,
"The stately limes", and the grass with little iron hoops
To stop a path being worn between them and the mound,
All this will be there when I return, surely all this?
And our sons, and the Germans' sons, will come in years
And know these things, and return to their homes, to fight –
Oh! rather than that, smash, fling them all down some night!

Note:
    Happy memories are stirred as he reads a poem, by one of his favourite poets, recalling the Oxford University life they both enjoyed.
    He mulls over the fate of friends, his homeland and the irony of returning home to see the names of those friends added to the long Roll of Honour. He cannot believe that those long lists of names from the Great War would now be extended by names with which he can identify.

Original drawing of part of Eichstaëtt camp showing the sites of nest boxes for the Redstart studies

The Apple-Trees

There are five apple-trees here, standing in a row:
One day, when the wind began to blow,
   I watched the petals falling
     Into the ditch below.

Beyond the wire is an orchard full of apple-trees:
One morning the petals fallen from these
   Were lying thickly strewn
     Over the grass below.

In my garden in England an apple-tree stands:
Today the petals are fluttering over her hands
   While she is gathering the bluebells
     And the celandines below.

Note:
    On a spring day in 1943, the sight of falling apple blossom transports John's thoughts back home to Marjorie gathering flowers.

Silhouette

5

The joy of battle – that I never knew
(The more's my loss), unless the joy should lie
In the curled, waiting finger, and watchful eye
Sifting each distant movement through and through.
But when that crawling shape came into view
Over the steady sights, what joy had I
To see it jerk, fling out an arm, and die?
What joy in such an easy thing to do?
Death I accept as man – who does not so?
And killing I accept at England's need.
I am not alone in war, but know
Myself as citizen. But none shall read
Of joy in battle in my verse and throw
That camouflage on men who lie and bleed.

August 19th 1942, Oflag VI B, Germany

Note:
    He admits killing a man – a very painful admission for him to make. There was no joy in it for him. He would not boast or jest as some other men did at such deeds – to him it was a terrible act.

Sonnet

I listened in the night: you spoke to me
   Softly, so very softly, one quiet word,
   Still sleeping; and your gentle breath I heard
Moving with the rhythm of the distant sea.
Moon-shadows, like the shadows in a tree,
   Fluttered about your breasts, or like a bird
   Flitting among green leaves. And then you stirred,
And oh! I saw your eyes, or seemed to see.
But seemed, oh! too beloved ghost, but seemed,
   For though I think I never saw more clear
   Your throat, your lips, your cheeks, your eyes that teemed
With longing, the crisp hair about your ear,
   The very way you waked – I merely dreamed
   And you are still alone, and nowhere near.

Note:
   In the quiet solitude of the night Marjorie comes to him in his thoughts; they are together in mind, if not in body.

Night Raiders

Night Raid

The bombers drum their way along the night
    With slow tattoo, down an invisible track
    Drawn on a map of Europe, which now lies black,
Huddled in silence. So, at mountain-height,
They tread their level path beyond our sight
    And pass relentlessly onward, flinging back
    The tramp of engines moving to attack
Enemy cities, to set their streets alight.
And we lie listening, hoping to hear the burst
    Of bombs in the crumbling houses, to hear the panes
Shivering in our windows. We shall be first
    To tot up the dead in the papers. (Someone explains
That this is a partial list.) We too have been cursed
      By the bombs; we have felt their pulses in all our
        veins.

Note:
   He describes his feelings as he lies awake listening to the Allied bombers passing overhead on another raid, and he hints that some raids had come dangerously close to their own camp!

8

If for a single hour I might be free
  And that one hour might all be spent with you,
  What should we say, my love? what should we do
In such a little hour as that would be?
Words, after so long, would not come to me;
  Kisses would be but torture, being so few
  And yet recalling all the joy we knew
Before I went to war beyond the sea.
But if I took you to the edge of land
  Where we might watch the sea spread wide away
  And the slant waves along the pebbles creep,
Then by the white brink of the tide we'd stand
  And press each other's hand, and nothing say,
  But know the silence coming from the deep.

Note:
Sent to Marjorie in the middle of winter 1942.
  Cold, hungry and parted from the one he loves; in such conditions it would have been a necessary virtue to retain the pleasure of anticipation, and to dream awhile.

"... white weals where they go ..."

Daylight Raid

Feet chip their hurried sound from the street, that
 gathers
Silence behind their heels and out of the porches
As soon as doors slam to. A still sparrow perches
There on the eaves and preens his dust-clogged
 feathers,
Shakes himself. Listen! bombers now the rent air throw
In gouts to our ears, cicatrize the breast of sky
That the sudden frost heals to white weals where they
 go,
And we know by their slow curve where the targets lie.
Far off guns inject the air with their grey serum
To disinfect the ground from the spasm of the bombs.
But we feel them shudder in our bones, a town strums
Dirges for falling walls on our nerves that raze them.

Note:
 The true naturalist! He notices that the noise and action of war do not concern the sparrow – who carries on preening himself regardless.
 A little piece of information is revealed in the line which shows how they are able to predict which town is being targeted.

The War Poems of John Buxton

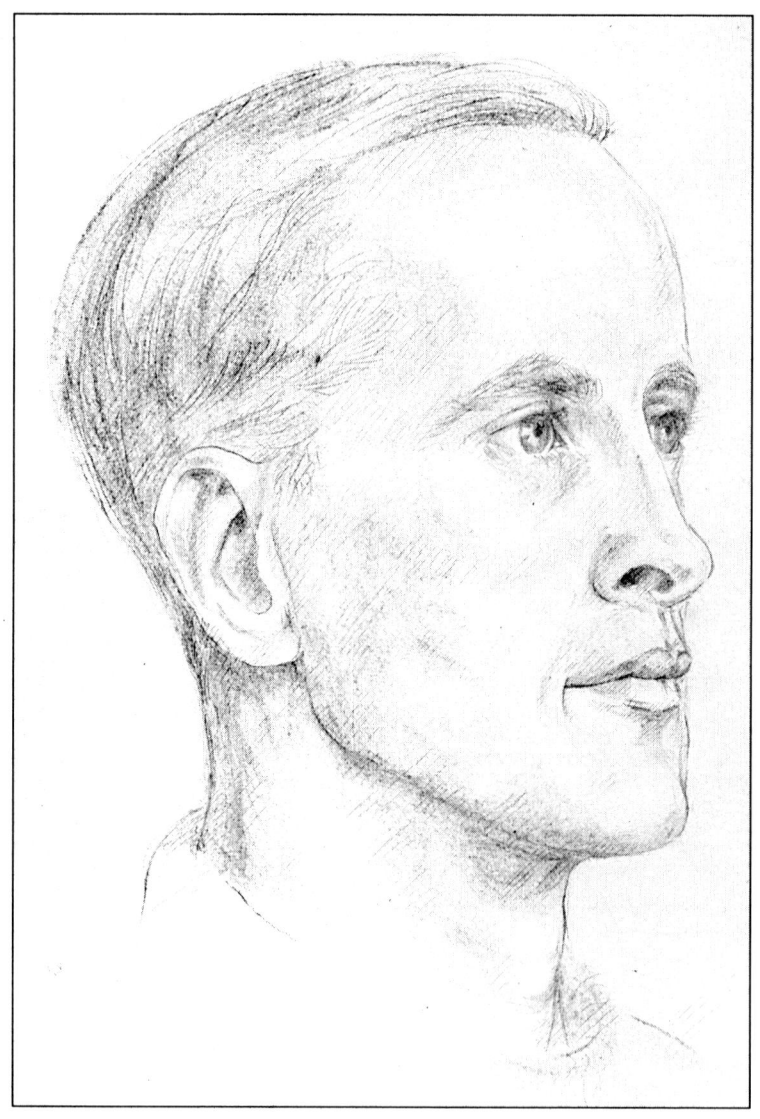

Line drawing of John Buxton, Eichstaëtt 1943

SONNETS

2

You'd think that I'd turned monk to see me now:
(God knows what Order such as me enlists!) –
The meagrest diet on which man exists –
Most ancient herrings, milk of long-dead cow, –
Gave this aesthetic pallor to my brow,
These knobbly fingers, and these bony wrists.
Insolent time on tonsure too insists.
I'm forced to chastity's discourteous vow.
Aye! even that! I'm one with Aberlard,
A poet gelded, or a monk forsworn,
- As you prefer; these sonnets all I'm left,
A cell wherein to ponder this canard
That I am hoaxed with, who am a thing of scorn
Being of love's sweet practices bereft.

Note:
There is almost a hint of a jest in the comparison of his prisoner status with that of a monk. Poor food, in poor physical condition, and pining for lost days of love.

Line drawing of Marjorie Buxton, Long Crendon, 1943

On Receiving Harold Speed's Portrait of M.B.

Though half a continent now lies
Between us or our meeting eyes;
And years have kept our lips away;
Nor can ears catch what voice would say,
And hand leans out in vain to hand
Across seven hundred miles of land;
Oh! more than memory is mine,
For here I see the very line
Of hair brushed off from ear and brow
To cluster at her neck, and how
The shadows lie beneath her chin,
The lips parted, the petal skin,
The white, cool throat. Here's all delight
Whether of touch or sound or sight! –
And that clear look that's in her eyes
Full of all loveliness, and wise
With secret things we two had found
When self to self no more was bound.
Oh! now she comes so near, so near
That even her longed-for voice I hear;
As if, far inland, one should find
A shell the tide had left behind
A million years ago, which he
Holds to his ear, and hears the sea.

(Note: overleaf)

The War Poems of John Buxton

Note:
   Harold Speed dated his portrait "1943" which implies that the sketch of John drawn in the camp and dated 14.2.43 probably acted as the catalyst for Marjorie to ask Harold Speed to draw her in return. The portrait carries the camp stamp on the reverse.

Prisoners Skating on the Frozen Ground at Eichstaëtt, Winter 1944. (Camp huts are in the background) (I.W.M. HU34265)

Walking in the Snow

I was in the far woods
    Where spruce trees throw
Still blue shadows
    That seep across the snow.
I was in the woods again
    Walking in the snow.

And there was silence:
    No voice spoke there,
No bird among the branches,
    No wind in the air,
No sleeping animal
    Stirred in its lair.

There was no bright blossom,
    No leaf or bud of green:
The snow's patterned crystals
    Were all that might be seen –
They split the silver sunlight
    Their glassy fronds between.

And I was alone again,
    With no one there to know
Where my last step was planted,
    Where my next must go.
I was in the far woods
    Walking in the snow.

(Note: overleaf)

The War Poems of John Buxton

Note:
 At Eichstaëtt, in the early months of 1944, prisoners were able to take walks outside the camp wire. They could walk into the woods beyond the little river. He has gained a little freedom, but finds himself still alone without even the company of a bird to share his walk in the snow.

THE WAR POEMS OF JOHN BUXTON

Willow Warbler

WILLOW WARBLER

I may walk in the woods now
Where the spears of grass
Thrust through the fallen leaves, and rain
Spills from the trees I pass.
I need not wait now till you come near
Nor grieve when you go where I cannot hear.

I may stand in the woods now
And lean by a tree.
Your fairy laughter I hear again;
In the breaking leaves I see
Where you go flitting above my head,
Free to follow wherever I'm led.

(Moosburg, Germany, 2nd May 1945; relieved 29th April)

Note:
   In the divide between full captivity and true freedom John tastes the simple delight of a walk in the woods. Spring has come again and he is happy to follow the Warbler's song.

"... where the long waves plunge toward me ..."

On Seeing The Sea For The First Time For Five Years

Not stained, not scarred by all man's history;
Wholly indifferent; without pity or pride
For battles fought there, and a world defied,
Or drowned men flung ashore quite carelessly;
This will not praise us for our victory,
Nor mock defeat, nor our quick moods deride,
But moon-driven for ever by mechanic tide
Will sweep about these coasts still heedlessly.
And while I watch each sinuous movement there,
And see the opal colours shift and fade
Where the long waves plunge toward me, I am glad,
Yes, glad that the land's whole history is in the care
Of this unhistoried thing, never dismayed
By all man has done that is evil, or cruel, or sad.

Note:
He is glad to see the sea again and to find that it remains unaffected by man and the tide of war.

Sonnets II

8

If men remember me when I am dead
I shall not be alone, but at my side
You shall for ever be with me, my dear bride
Turning toward me your small inquiring head.
They'll overhear some of the things we said
When we lay in the sun together, and watched the tide
Crawling below us, and they'll know my pride
And smile with you – and think of you instead.
And yet, how very little will they know
Who never heard you speak, nor saw your face,
Nor watched the laughter dance in your eyes.
How should I tell the ways the wind would blow
The hair from cheek or nape? the deer-like grace
That in your body's sweet enclosure lies?

Note:
It is not known when he wrote this poem, but it was printed in *Such Liberty* in 1944. It is another example of his deep affection and love for Marjorie. It nearly opens the door to the private feelings and thoughts of those we love, which we guard closely.

Epilogue

To quote from his obituary in *The Times*, "strongly built, darkly handsome and intelligent, sensitive to the point of seeming to have fewer skins than other men, Buxton issued three clear and beautiful books of verse and did not 'sing' again. He returned with clipped wings from his captivity, subdued in manner, nervous and intense, where before he had been bold and responsive."

In 1946 he collapsed and was diagnosed as suffering from diabetes, which would require him to inject himself with insulin every day for the rest of his life. Diabetes was instrumental in preventing he and his wife Marjorie from having a family of their own. He later lost an eye from suspected cancer.

After the war he returned to Oxford to become a Language Don. He wrote several books on the English Renaissance. These were scholarly works, no longer the intense cry of a poet unable to remain silent. John became a respected Fellow of New College, but with lasting damage to both body and soul, such a man should be remembered as one of many undecorated heroes and the unknown victims of war.